DR ANTHONY GUNN

GET HAPPY!

LESSONS IN LASTING HAPPINESS

hardie grant books

Published in 2015 by Hardie Grant Books,
an imprint of Hardie Grant Publishing

Hardie Grant Books (Melbourne)
Building 1, 658 Church Street
Richmond, Victoria 3121
hardiegrantbooks.com.au

Hardie Grant Books (London)
5th & 6th Floor
52–54 Southwark Street
London SE1 1UN
hardiegrantbooks.co.uk

A Cataloguing-in-Publication entry is available from the catalogue
of the National Library of Australia at www.nla.gov.au
Get Happy!
ISBN 978 1 74379 006 9

Cover design by Kinart
Text design by Patrick Cannon
Typeset in Granjon 11.5/16 pt by Cannon Typesetting
Author photo courtesy of Handprint Photography

Printed and bound in China by 1010 Printing International Limited

To my brothers, Mick and Ian,
and my sister Kazz,
for always being there.

1. The science of happiness

Can we really become happier or is happiness determined by our genes? Researchers have found that 50 per cent of our happiness is determined by genes and only 10 per cent by what happens to us in our lives. Amazingly, this means 40 per cent of our happiness is within our control. In spite of what you have inherited or what tragedies you have experienced in life, there are things you can do to increase your happiness. Continue reading to learn the lessons of lasting happiness.

'The basic root of happiness lies in our minds; outer circumstances are nothing more than adverse or favourable.'
— Matthieu Ricard

2. Need versus want

Most of us in developed countries have all our basic needs met: food, shelter, hygiene, safety and education. So we have to rely on wants to make us happy, such as wanting a new car, new lounge, bigger TV, newer phone. Sadly, our wants will never make us happy in the long term because we don't need them to survive. Tap back into your basic needs. For example:

- *Thirst:* Do a physical challenge that causes you to develop a real thirst, and notice how good a drink of water tastes.
- *Safety:* Feel a buzz of exhilaration by taking a small risk, such as doing a difficult water activity or holding a tame snake at a zoo.
- *Warmth:* Have a cold shower in cold weather and then focus on getting warm.

Happiness is appreciating the things we most *need*.

'*Wealth consists not in having great possessions, but in having few wants.*'
— Epictetus

3. Habituation, the villain of happiness

Do you like chocolate? The first piece of chocolate will taste great, yet each subsequent piece will offer decreasing pleasure. Why? It's because we get used to things; in psychology, this is called habituation. You think you'll be happy once you get that new car, renovated kitchen, polished floorboards or whatever, but the happiness won't last long because the novelty wears off. The result is that you need to buy another new object to try to increase your happiness again. Before buying a new non-essential object, ask yourself how long it will keep you happy.

'An object in possession seldom retains the same charm that it had in pursuit.'
— Pliny the Younger

4. Finding happiness in discomfort

If habituation causes us to become used to things quickly, what is the answer to finding lasting happiness? Variety really is the best defence against habituation. A good way to practise this is by stepping out of your comfort zone, by trying a new sport, meeting new people, going to new places, learning a new skill or furthering your education. Every time you step out of your comfort zone, you're forced to grow as a person. Make *yourself* the focus of change instead of changing objects around you and watch your happiness rise.

'Nothing builds self-esteem and self-confidence like accomplishment.'
– Thomas Carlyle

---

5. Focus on your body's ability instead of its image

Research shows that a number of people who undergo elective cosmetic surgery still think they look ugly afterwards, regardless of their new appearance. Likewise, glamorous beauty contestants frequently obsess about not being pretty enough, and muscle-bound bodybuilders worry they should be more muscular. Want to be happy with your body? Instead of focusing on what's wrong with it and comparing yourself to others, focus on what your body can do. What things has your body allowed you to accomplish in life?

> *'Your body is not a temple,*
> *it's an amusement park.*
> *Enjoy the ride.'*
> — ANTHONY BOURDAIN

6. Flexibly happy

A key feature of many types of mental health issues is that the suffering person is inflexible to change. Change is all around us. Simply by reading this book you will have changed. Instead of trying to fight the inevitable, embrace change – one of the keys to happiness. Change doesn't have to be negative; it can offer variety, novelty, surprise and excitement. Try making small changes in your life: try a new fashion, rearrange the furniture in your home or office, try a new food, or skip for the fun of it. Once you get used to making small changes, bigger ones will seem possible. Go on, embrace change and become flexibly happy!

*'The key to sustained happiness,
health, and longevity is flexibility.'*
– EV DURÁN

7. Smiling makes you look sexy

You may think that a fashion model sporting a serious look is appealing to others, but research would say the opposite. A team from the University of Bern in Switzerland found that when people were asked to evaluate a face, what made the face appear attractive was the intensity of its smile. Evolutionary psychologists believe this is because when we smile we are indicating to others that we are healthy and free of illness. What's more, smiling helps release the feel-good hormones dopamine and serotonin in the body, making us feel better. Try this experiment: for one whole day try smiling, especially if you are not feeling in the mood, and see what happens to your happiness.

'Smile, it's free therapy.'
– Douglas Horton

8. Count your blessings

Researchers have found that regularly counting your blessings increases happiness. Try the experiment researchers used: for one week, set aside ten minutes each night before you go to bed to write down three things that went well that day. You have to physically write it down on paper or type it on your computer, instead of just doing the exercise in your head. Next to each positive event in your list, answer the question, 'Why did this good thing happen?' The researchers found that not only did this make people happier, but the benefits lasted for six months. Give it a go!

'Don't cry because it's over.
Smile because it happened.'
– Dr Seuss

9. What are the most valuable things in your life?

How would you feel if you lost everything? I recently spoke with a gentleman, Gordon, who had just lost everything in a bushfire: house, business, workshop, cars, family photos, all gone. Yet, despite this tragedy, he remained optimistic and happy. How is this possible? Gordon said that when everything was taken by the fire, he was able to focus on what was most important in life, and it wasn't material objects. Instead, he said it was family, friends and reputations. It's sobering to imagine how we'd react to losing everything we own. What are the most valuable things in *your* life?

---

*'The things you own end up owning you.
It's only after you lose everything
that you're free to do anything.'*
— Fight Club, Chuck Palahniuk

---

10. Give a compliment

Making someone else happy can make you feel great. Give someone you know a compliment. Seeing their happiness will be contagious. However, if they are the type who won't accept compliments ('No, anyone could bake a cake like mine'), then you need to get under their guard. A clever way to get past these defences is to pass on a compliment someone else has given them. For example, you could say, 'Sally was raving about your chocolate cake at last night's meeting.' It's harder to knock back a compliment that way because you're simply the messenger, and they'll feel more comfortable accepting it. Go on, give a compliment and notice how happy you feel.

'Everybody likes a compliment.'
– ABRAHAM LINCOLN

11. The dangers of hoarding

Do you have things that need to be thrown out, but you just can't bear to let them go? At its extreme, people surround themselves with objects; it's known as hoarding. Unconsciously, they believe the objects bring them happiness and that discarding them would result in emotional pain. Some researchers suggest that people develop relationships with objects to make up for a lack of human relationships in their lives. Are you relying on objects to bring you happiness? What objects can you let go of? Replace your possessions with people and watch your happiness increase.

'Treasure your relationships,
not your possessions.'
– ANTHONY J D'ANGELO

12. Regret is toxic for happiness

The more choices you have, the harder it is to choose. We fear making the wrong decision and then having to live with regret. Regret is unlike any other negative emotion because it makes us think something could have been avoided if we had chosen differently. The more options we have, the greater the chance of regret. If there's a long queue at the checkout because it's the only one open, it will be annoying but there will be no regret. However, if there are two checkouts, both with queues, and you get stuck behind a slow customer, you might regret choosing the wrong queue. A simple way to avoid regret and increase happiness is to reduce the number of options before making a decision.

'Never look back unless you are planning to go that way.'
– HENRY DAVID THOREAU

13. There's happiness in having rules

To avoid regret fuelled by indecision, limit your choices by having simple rules to live by for everyday decisions. The following are some examples:

- Simplify your schedule; what can you say no to?
- Give yourself a set amount of time to think about a person's request before responding.
- Have a place for everything, and if it doesn't have a place, get rid of it.
- Be early to appointments.
- Only go shopping after you've eaten.

Indecision is the breeding ground for regret. Develop simple rules ahead of time for avoiding indecision and stress, and put this saved energy towards your happiness.

'Failing to plan is planning to fail.'
– ALAN LAKEIN

14. What's your noise pollution?

The rock band AC/DC had a hit song that claimed *'Rock and Roll Ain't Noise Pollution'*. Some may argue as to what noise pollution is, though many people are not aware of its damaging effects. Research shows that children's learning is impaired when schools are next to noisy environments such as airports or construction work. Noise pollution affects happiness because it prevents you from being able to fully concentrate on a task at hand. Avoid studying with the TV on, try noise-cancelling headphones with soothing music if you're working in a noisy office, and maybe postpone that deep and meaningful conversation with a friend if kids are demanding your attention at the time. What noise pollution can you reduce in your life?

'Silence is a source of great strength.'
– LAO TZU

15. Get off the worry-wheel

Worry is a happiness killer. Do you often keep going over problems in your mind that you can't solve? This is known as rumination. Whether you're worrying about what people think, financial issues, or the wellbeing of family members, ruminating on problems will risk happiness. What's worse is that it often feels good, like we are fixing the problem, but this is a trap. Rumination is similar to a hamster on a wheel: you put in lots of work but go nowhere. Break the wheel of worry through action. What can you physically do about the problem? If everything has been done, then distract yourself from the problem by doing activities that bring enjoyment. Starting today, what can you do to get off the worry-wheel?

'We either make ourselves miserable,
or we make ourselves strong.
The amount of work is the same.'
— CARLOS CASTANEDA

16. Can you buy happiness?

Yes, you can buy happiness, but only to a degree.
Once the basic essentials are met, money doesn't
appear to increase happiness. Research shows
that the more money a person has, the more
they believe they'll need to stay happy. A study
showed that those who earned less than $30,000
a year said that $50,000 would fulfil their dreams,
whereas those earning more than $100,000 said
they'd need $250,000 to make them happy. The
people who were struggling financially were given
a questionnaire asking what they would need to
make them happy; when they were financially
secure years later they were given the same
questionnaire, and their happiness levels barely
differed. Once your basic needs for living are met,
focus on your relationships and social events, such
as holidays and hobbies, for your main source
of happiness.

'Too many people spend money they haven't earned, to buy things they don't want, to impress people they don't like.'

— WILL ROGERS

17. Will winning the lottery make you happier?

If you think you would be happier if you won the lottery, think again. Lottery winners can end up unhappy, depressed and poor. The more we have to work for something, the more we will appreciate it, and the more likely it will bring us happiness. Yet, winning the lottery offers the total opposite. Resist the urge to believe that once you win the lottery, you'll be happy. This type of thinking robs you of taking control of your life now, and forces you to live in hope of something that is unlikely to ever happen.

'When you get something for nothing, you just haven't been billed for it yet.'
— FRANKLIN P JONES

18. Eating before bed

Do you eat just before going to bed? Many people do, but risk lowering their happiness because eating late affects sleep. The digestive system is controlled by the body's circadian rhythms, or the body's 24-hour clock, which respond to light and darkness. During the night, digestion slows down irrespective of the body's activity. Where possible, avoid eating at least one hour before bed. You'll sleep better without a busy stomach, which in turn will increase your happiness.

'A child, like your stomach, doesn't need all you can afford to give it.'
– Frank A Clark

19. Walk happy

A recent scientific study measured people's brain activity as they watched faceless, computer-animated people walk. The participants had to guess what emotion the animated characters were feeling based on their walk. Not only did the people in the study correctly identify the emotion, but negative emotional walks such as fearful or angry walks were more easily identified, and showed increased neural activity in the participants' brain scans. Maybe there is some truth in the idea that people's body language projects an aura. If you want people to see you in a positive and happy light, then walk happy.

'A good stance and posture reflect
a proper state of mind.'
– Morihei Ueshiba

20. I'll know I'm successful when …

This is a simple statement, though one that few of us make. For example, you may think you'll be successful when you're a millionaire, own a certain type of car or live in a certain type of house or area. But then what? Remember, habituation will quickly make materialistic gains seem mediocre at best. Instead, focus on making a difference in others' lives. It may be raising happy and confident children, working for a worthy cause or leaving some kind of a legacy. Go on, complete the statement, 'I'll know I'm successful when …'

'Remember that "He who dies with the most toys wins" is a bumper sticker, not wisdom.'
— BARRY SCHWARTZ

21. Success doesn't equal happiness

A common way of thinking is that success amounts to happiness. For example, if a person works harder, then they'll be more successful, and if they become more successful, they'll be happier. The problem with this logic is that every time you succeed you have to change the goalposts. It is often said that actors, athletes or business people are only as good as their last performance. Maybe you did well in your last test, but now have an expectation to maintain this high level. Maybe your sales targets were reached, but then were increased to keep pushing you. Success is one measure of our achievements, but it's also a dangerous illusion if you believe it's the only gauge of happiness. Does what you do truly make you happy? If yes, then you are a success. If no, then it may be time to re-evaluate your goals.

'Success is not the key to happiness.
Happiness is the key to success.
If you love what you are doing,
you will be successful.'

— ALBERT SCHWEITZER

22. What makes a successful couple?

The sign of a happy couple is that they never argue, right? Wrong! Research shows that couples who never fight have a higher risk of separation, as it's likely that one person in the relationship is suppressing their emotions to keep the peace. Successful couples do clash, but it's all about the way they fight. They fight fairly without personally attacking their partner, and instead focus on their partner's behaviour. Compare 'I didn't like the way you controlled the TV remote' with 'You are a selfish, self-centred moron'. Whether it's your partner, child, friend or work colleague, if you want to raise an issue with them, focus on addressing their behaviour instead of attacking them personally. Successful relationships are at the heart of happiness. Learn to look after yours.

*'The only normal people are the ones
you don't know very well.'*
— Alfred Adler

23. Learn another language

Research has found that crosswords and other puzzles may not be as effective for deterring dementia as was once thought. Better options are tasks that are difficult to master, things that you'll feel like giving up on, such as learning a new language. Dedicate ten to fifteen minutes a day to learning a language or, if you're really serious, do an evening course. Not only will your brain thank you for it, but mastering a skill like this will increase your confidence, thereby increasing your happiness.

> *'To have another language
> is to possess a second soul.'*
>
> — CHARLEMAGNE

24. Learn to release tension

Many of us are regularly stressed, and therefore our muscles are constantly tense. Being relaxed brings happiness, but trying to relax can be hard. Approach the problem from a different angle: deliberately become tense. Tense your feet for five seconds and then relax. Next, tense your legs and relax. Do this all the way up to your jaw. Your muscles will find it easier to relax themselves, and it's also a powerful technique that you can use any time, anywhere. Learn to be tense and get happy.

'The time to relax is when you don't have time for it.'
— Sydney J Harris

25. Hold hands with your anxiety

Helpful anxiety is good because it motivates us to act. For example, research shows that moderate anxiety motivates women to get regular mammogram scans, whereas women with low anxiety levels don't worry about the tests. With too much anxiety we freeze, and with too little we become complacent. Yet we perform best with a degree of anxiety, as the graph below illustrates.

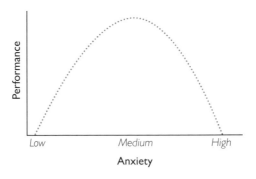

How do you make anxiety helpful? Instead of trying to get rid of your anxiety, learn to see it as a friend or a scared child, and hold its hand. Whenever you step out of a comfort zone, expect to feel some anxiety. Being friends with your anxiety and holding its hand will allow you to perform at your best and become a happier person.

'There is no such thing as pure pleasure; some anxiety always goes with it.'
— OVID

26. What are you holding on to?

Two monks were returning to the monastery in the rain when they saw a beautiful young woman unable to cross the muddy road. The elder monk lifted the woman and carried her to the other side of the road, where the woman thanked him profusely. The elder monk just smiled and then continued on his journey to the monastery. Much later the younger monk said to the elder monk, 'You should not have picked that woman up as you could have been tempted.' The elder monk smiled at him and said, 'I left her on the other side of the road, but you are still carrying her.'

What are you needlessly holding on to that's robbing you of happiness?

'In the end, just three things matter:
How well we have lived;
How well we have loved;
How well we have learned to let go.'

— JACK KORNFIELD

27. Claim small victories

A great way to boost happiness is to be aware of every time you have a small win. If you get two green lights in a row, smile. Find a parking spot in a busy shopping centre: victory. Asked to go to a newly opened checkout at the supermarket, making you first in the line: winner! Make yourself aware of these small victories and take joy in them. This will strengthen your happiness.

'Winning isn't everything,
but the will to win is everything.'
— Vince Lombardi

28. Drown-proofing fear

Imagine having your ankles bound and your hands tied behind your back before being thrown into a swimming pool. Sounds horrific! This is what soldiers seeking to qualify for the elite US Navy Seals are forced to go through. The logic is that it teaches soldiers to overcome their initial panic and discover that they can indeed swim when bound. I use this example not so you'll try this, but to show what can be achieved once fear is controlled. We humans are far more resilient than we often give ourselves credit for. We can't get rid of fear, but we can learn to embrace it. A fear that controls you will also control your happiness. What small fear can you embrace and master?

'The cave you fear to enter holds the treasure you seek.'
— Joseph Campbell

29. Question your judgements

Try this brainteaser: a bat and ball cost $1.10. The bat costs $1 more than the ball. How much is the ball?

If you said the ball costs 10 cents, you have fallen into a common trap that also catches many top university students. If the ball was 10 cents then the bat (to be worth $1 more than the ball) would have to cost $1.10, and this totals $1.20. The correct answer is the ball would cost 5 cents (5 cents + $1.05 = $1.10).

The reason we make this common mistake is that our brains look for the easiest option and then latch on to it as a way of saving time and energy. The next time you make a quick negative judgement about either another person or yourself, pause. Often happiness is found when we are prepared to accept that our opinions may not be correct, especially opinions about what we think we can't do.

'The measure of intelligence is the ability to change.'
— ALBERT EINSTEIN

30. Become a photographer

Many years ago I saw a woman for counselling who suffered from such debilitating social anxiety that she would go over each sentence in her mind before speaking out loud, as she was scared of saying something embarrassing. Yet, surprisingly, she was a successful wedding photographer. How? Because her focus was on her environment instead of herself. Take a camera and start taking photos of your environment. You will be amazed at what you start noticing, and it's also a great way to discover new places and step out of your comfort zone, especially if you're shy. Not only will your happiness increase, but you may also uncover a hidden talent!

'The camera is an instrument that teaches people how to see without a camera.'
– DOROTHEA LANGE

31. Change things by 1 per cent

There's an old saying that if you want to increase your performance by 100 per cent, then change one hundred small things that you do by 1 per cent each. Often we think we have to make big sacrifices for change to occur. The problem is the bigger the change, the bigger the risk of going back to what's familiar. This is why radical diets don't work in the long term. Instead, make small changes to your lifestyle. Walk the stairs instead of taking the lift, have a piece of fruit before eating an unhealthy snack, or go to bed ten minutes earlier if you're always feeling tired. Often it's the small changes that make the big differences to happiness. What small change have you been putting off?

'A year from now you will wish you had started today.'
– KAREN LAMB

---

32. Be mindful and do a 'present' activity

When we think about the future, anxiety can be triggered; when we think about the past we can feel depressed. But when we focus on the present moment, it's impossible to feel anxiety or depression. A great way to focus on the present is to use mindfulness meditation. This is a type of meditation where you can do things while meditating at the same time. The key is to focus on one of your five senses: sight, sound, smell, taste or touch. For example, next time you're walking, notice how your feet feel with each step you take. Try this challenge: dedicate thirty seconds to each one of your five senses. You might start with sight. What five things can you see? After thirty seconds move to your next sense. Follow the same pattern for hearing, touch, smell and taste. Being mindful for short periods of time can reduce stress quickly, which is great news for happiness.

'If you aren't in the moment, you are either looking forward to uncertainty, or back to pain and regret.'

— JIM CARREY

33. Eat mindfully

Food can make us either happy or sad. One chocolate biscuit is wonderful; a whole packet can be depressing. Do you ever find yourself eating for comfort, yet the more you eat, the more distressed you become? Next time you notice yourself eating for comfort, take your time and eat slowly. Enjoy each bite and savour it. Eating mindfully not only brings comfort and happiness, but also means we require far less food as we become full more quickly.

'The more you eat, the less flavour;
the less you eat, the more flavour.'
— CHINESE PROVERB

34. Are you 'fortune telling' your happiness away?

Experts have been shown to be extremely bad at making predictions about the future. Yet they aren't the only ones who get forecasts wrong. We often fall into the trap of negatively predicting how we will perform: *I won't go for the job because I won't get it*; *No-one will talk to me at the party*; *I could never learn to dance.* Anticipating that things might turn out badly, then believing that this assumption is an already established fact is a guaranteed way to lower happiness. Find out for yourself. For one week, keep a diary of the negative future predictions you make for yourself, and then see if they really come true. Go on, I dare you.

---

*'Every day I make predictions
that don't come anywhere close to the mark.'*
— JOE POSNANSKI

---

35. Rely less on willpower

A key to being happy is making positive changes to your environment. How does your environment fuel your bad habits? For example, do you want to eat healthier but keep junk food in the cupboard? With temptation in your kitchen you must force yourself not to eat the junk food. The key is to go easy on yourself by not having the temptation there in the first place. Otherwise, once you tire, so will your willpower, and you'll eat the food you're not meant to. As a result you will feel like a failure. Happy people avoid setting themselves up for failure. What temptations can you remove from your home?

'Your goal is not to have more willpower.
Your goal is to need less willpower.'
– TODD FLEISCHER AND JERRY BOCKOVEN

36. Become a master at avoiding unnecessary stress

How can you avoid unnecessary stress? The goal is to pre-empt stressful situations before they happen. Here are some examples:

- Avoid keeping stockpiles of junk food or alcohol in the house.
- Pause before saying yes to someone's request (or give a time frame for when you'll let them know).
- Avoid driving on a near-empty tank of fuel.
- Pay bills on time.

'Stress is nothing more than a socially acceptable form of mental illness.'
– RICHARD CARLSON

37. Avoiding avoidance

A wonderful source of happiness can be to empower yourself by breaking out of your comfort zone, especially in an area that has previously beaten you. In a cruel experiment, a dog was put in a cage, where it learned the hard way that the red half of the floor was electrified and the green half wasn't. Every day for a year, the dog was placed back in the cage, without electricity, and only for a short period of time. The dog never walked on the red section again, despite the floor no longer being electrified. What uncomfortable experience have you had in life that you will never return to? Maybe it was driving in unfavourable conditions, having your idea knocked back in a meeting, or dating after being in an unhealthy relationship. Try breaking out of your comfort zone, because you'll never know something is safe unless you revisit it.

'Opposition is a natural part of life. Just as we develop our physical muscles through overcoming opposition – such as lifting weights – we develop our character muscles by overcoming challenges and adversity.'

– STEPHEN R COVEY

38. How often do you read?

One of the greatest gifts a person can have is the ability to read, as it can be an amazing source of happiness, either through education or as an escape. What are things that bring you happiness that you can read about? Here is a challenge: before bed each night or when travelling on public transport, spend ten to fifteen minutes reading something you enjoy. Make reading a pleasure instead of a chore and watch your happiness soar.

'You don't have to burn books to destroy a culture. Just get people to stop reading them.'
— RAY BRADBURY

39. Grow food

People waste a lot of money by throwing out uneaten food. Ways to control food wastage include buying food once the majority of perishable items in the fridge have been eaten, planning your meals ahead of time and only buying what you need for those meals, and growing your own food. Not only is it very satisfying, but when we grow food ourselves we are less likely to waste it because we've helped create it. Even if they're just herbs, being able to grow and then eat food is a very primal and fulfilling part of life. It's also a great way to reconnect with the environment, something that has been shown to increase happiness.

'He who plants a garden plants happiness.'
— GERMAN PROVERB

40. Care for a plant

If growing your own food is not something you can realistically see yourself doing, then focus on looking after a plant instead. Research shows that caring for a plant helps increase happiness, and also increases work productivity and air quality if kept in an office. Plant care helps lower blood pressure, decreases anxiety during recovery from surgery, and has even been shown to help elderly people live longer. There are many different types of indoor plants to choose from. One type of plant that can bring a lot of pleasure is a bonsai tree, as growing one is also an art form. Adopt a plant. A small plant could be a big investment in your happiness.

*'Just because you've only got houseplants
doesn't mean you don't have the gardening spirit –
I look upon myself as an indoor gardener.'*
— SARA MOSS-WOLFE

41. Be aware of the *'I used to'* syndrome

You've probably heard fit and able people say things such as:

- I used to go fishing.
- I used to go camping.
- I used to go dancing.
- I used to exercise.
- I used to socialise more.

If a person still wants and is physically able to do an activity that previously gave them enjoyment, but chooses not to, then it's time for concern. The moment a person uses the words 'I used to', they have an under-investment in their physical and emotional wellbeing. If you find yourself using the 'I used to' statement, stop and take stock of your life because it's likely you're putting your own needs way down the priority list. Make happiness a priority by replacing *I used to* with *I will*.

'Happiness is not something ready made.
It comes from your own actions.'
— Dalai Lama

42. Have something to look forward to

One strong predictor of mental resilience in the face of hardship is having something to look forward to in the near future. It doesn't have to be a big thing, just something that sparks your curiosity and interest. This may be seeing a movie or show, having lunch with a friend, exploring somewhere new, expecting an item in the post, or going on a holiday. Make sure you have something to look forward to. It's cheap insurance against unhappiness.

'Planning is bringing the future into the present so that you can do something about it now.'
— ALAN LAKEIN

43. The primal fear of loss

What do you place more importance on: the possibility of gaining a reward, or of losing it? Research suggests the fear of loss is a stronger motivator. For example, most people would prefer a surgeon tell them that their upcoming operation has a 90 per cent chance of success, rather than a 10 per cent chance of failure. We are more motivated by the fear of loss than the hope of gain. What experiences are you missing out on because you fear you could lose something, instead of thinking of the happiness you could gain?

'An investment said to have an 80% chance of success sounds far more attractive than one with a 20% chance of failure. The mind can't easily recognize that they are the same.'

– Daniel Kahneman

44. Treating the primal fear of loss

Naturally, you don't want to shut off from the fear of loss. For example, many people with gambling addictions have distorted optimistic perceptions of what they can gain with their next bet. Your goal is to focus on everyday things that are safe. Focus on areas where you can gain, such as extra study, a new career, meeting new people, starting a new friendship, exercising, or changing your diet. The fear of loss will cripple you, keeping you in your comfort zone. Focus instead on what you could gain if you were to step out of your comfort zone, and feel your happiness increase.

'Twenty years from now you will be more disappointed by the things that you didn't do than by the ones you did do. So throw off the bowlines. Sail away from the safe harbor. Catch the trade winds in your sails. Explore. Dream. Discover.'

— MARK TWAIN

45. Let each day happily scare you

Anxiety lives in the unknown. This is why people often gain a sense of security from staying in uncomfortable but known situations: you remain in an unhealthy job or relationship, never show anyone the book you've written, don't replace clothes or objects when it's clearly necessary. The common mantra to justify such decisions is 'Better the devil you know', which could also be interpreted as 'I'm too scared to face the unknown'. Gain comes about by embracing the unknown. Each day there are endless possibilities for how you could achieve this. Act differently: have a conversation with a stranger, go to the movies by yourself, learn how to repair a small object that needs fixing, offer to take on a new challenge at work or delegate a job if you're doing too much. Embracing the unknown is scary, but it's also where happiness lives. What can you do to be happily scared today?

*'The reason people find it so hard to be happy
is that they always see the past better than
it was, the present worse than it is,
and the future less resolved than it will be.'*
— MARCEL PAGNOL

46. To change someone, first understand them

It's human nature to hold personal beliefs about how the world and other people should operate. It can motivate us to want to change other people if we feel their beliefs clash with ours. But trying to change a person's habits or beliefs is likely to be faced with resistance. Understand where a person is coming from by listening to them and asking non-confronting questions. Be genuinely interested. Simply allowing a person to express their beliefs can often help them see these same beliefs differently in their own mind. Or even better, it may allow you to reconsider your own beliefs, especially the ones that may be controlling your happiness.

'To save a man's life against his will is the same as killing him.'
– Quintus Horatius Flaccus Horace

47. Pay your social debts

I'm not talking about being in debt with financial institutions, but rather being in debt with people you know. The discomfort of feeling indebted to others can be a drain on happiness. Have you been helped by someone you know, but not returned the favour? Maybe they babysat your kids or gave you a lift. It's important to return the favour where possible: offer to mind their kids or reciprocate hospitality. If you can't repay the debt in this way, then consider giving a small gift. Remember, it doesn't matter what the gift is. What's important is that you acknowledge their help, to show you aren't taking them for granted. Have you paid all your social debts?

'Debts are like children: the smaller they are
the more noise they make.'

— SPANISH PROVERB

48. Are you sleep-drunk?

Did you know that after being awake for seventeen hours, your body will respond similarly to having a 0.05 blood alcohol level? Being awake for twenty hours is the same as having a 0.1 blood alcohol level. Being sleep deprived will make you stupid, and getting enough sleep (seven to eight hours a night) is highly effective for mental sharpness and attaining happiness. Yet many of us prefer staying up late, watching TV or using computers, so we don't feel cheated out of having time for ourselves. Try this experiment: for one week make getting to bed on time your priority and see how well you function. It will be worth it.

'Life's hard. It's even harder when you're stupid.'
— JOHN WAYNE

49. Are you suffering from performance problems?

The danger of not getting enough sleep is that it lowers your ability to perform well. People who are sleep deprived aren't able to gauge their own level of impairment so they often aren't aware that they are no longer functioning well. Sleep deprivation can have awful impacts on the body by:

- slowing your reaction time
- reducing your ability to communicate effectively
- dulling your memory
- reducing your ability to estimate risks.

Aim for seven to eight hours of sleep a night. If you see an improvement in your performance (which you will), your happiness will automatically increase.

'One hour's sleep before midnight
is better than two after it.'
— GERMAN PROVERB

50. Eat low-GI foods

If you want to look after your happiness, ensure your energy levels remain consistent by having more low-GI foods in your diet.

The glycaemic index (GI) ranks foods containing carbohydrates according to their effect on a person's blood sugar levels. (Blood sugar is what gives us energy to perform tasks and fend off fatigue.) High-GI foods are digested and absorbed quickly, causing a quick increase in blood sugar levels, followed by a quick drop. A sugar rush after eating chocolate is a great example: an instant high followed by an instant low. However, low-GI foods take longer to digest and be absorbed, resulting in longer-lasting energy. Lack of energy is linked to low mood, so the less energy you have, the less happy you'll probably be. Think of high-GI foods as sprinters and low-GI foods as marathon runners, and choose the slower burn.

*'The food you eat can be either the safest
and most powerful form of medicine
or the slowest form of poison.'*
— ANN WIGMORE

51. Being a workaholic kills happiness

People who are workaholics often place their self-worth on being needed at work, and are at a higher risk of suffering from mental health issues. Are you a focused person or simply a workaholic? If your life revolves solely around your work, change it. What hobbies could you take up? What places could you visit? Who can you reconnect with? Happiness is about having more than just work in your life. There is more to you than your job.

*'No one ever said on their deathbed
"I wish I'd spent more time at the office."'*
– HAROLD KUSHNER

52. Is something biological affecting your happiness?

There are factors that can affect a person's happiness besides their thoughts. If you've ever been hungry or thirsty, then you'll probably remember being irritable and fixated on food or water. Likewise, happiness can be affected by conditions such as menopause, period pain, physical pain, illness, disease and other medical problems. Have regular health checks to rule out unknown physical factors that may be preventing you from reaching your full happiness potential.

'The good physician treats the disease; the great physician treats the patient who has the disease.'

– William Osler

---

53. Be a teacher

Whether or not you feel you are smart, you have unique knowledge in a particular area that others could benefit from. What have you learned that you feel could help other people? It may be tips on home or car maintenance, cooking, gardening, sport, health, shopping or travel advice. You could share your knowledge by offering to do voluntary work, teaching a sport, art or hobby, or writing a blog. Knowing you're helping others is extremely gratifying. How can you be a teacher to benefit others?

'Even if you're not a teacher, be a teacher. Share your ideas.

— TIM MINCHIN

54. What gets you positively passionate?

Most people will be quick to tell others what they don't like or are against – whether it's a political party, music band or movie – which is what helps identify them as a person. Instead, let people know what you *do* like. What things are you grateful for? What things are you positively passionate about? Talk about what gets you positively passionate and not only will it make you happier, but your happiness will be contagious.

'Passion is energy. Feel the power that comes from focusing on what excites you.'
— OPRAH WINFREY

55. Have a will

Death is a subject that scares many of us. To talk about wills may seem in conflict with being happy, but it's only when we embrace our mortality, knowing that our time on earth is limited, that we become more aware of making the most of every day. Writing a will often helps you consider two vital questions: who are the important people in your life, and what will you leave them? It's confronting, but it's also freeing. Remember, happiness is based largely on the relationships in our lives. Who would you include in your will?

'The real tragedy of the poor is the poverty of their aspirations.'
— ADAM SMITH

56. Stretch daily

Regular stretching is just as important as exercise. Why? Stretching decreases both muscle tension and chances of injury, speeds up recovery from an injury, increases circulation and potentially helps slow the ageing process, to name but a few of the benefits. Regular stretching is one of the easiest ways to help look after your body. Stretch your arms and wrists while sitting at the computer, or stretch your legs while brushing your teeth. Incorporate stretching into your everyday life and you'll notice an amazing difference in how your body feels. A healthy body makes for a happy person.

'… we bend or we break.'
– KELLY G WILSON

57. Do you have a choice?

Some people continue to make the same mistakes, such as going from one unhealthy relationship to another, failing to maintain an exercise or diet regime, or continuing to get into unhealthy debt. These people say these are mistakes they've made, but repeatedly making the same mistake is not a mistake, it's a choice. Knowing that we have the ability to choose may seem self-defeating, but taking ownership of the decisions we make becomes empowering. Taking back control increases happiness. Do you have a little more control over your life than you previously believed?

'You can't make the same mistake twice.
The second time you make it,
it's no longer a mistake. It's a choice.'
– Steven Denn

58. Monitor your narcissism

In recent research, psychologists studied hit songs over a three-decade period and found the frequency of lyrics containing 'I' and 'me' increased along with words related to self-focus and antisocial behaviour. They also found a corresponding decline in the use of 'we' and 'us' and words related to focusing on others, social interactions and positive emotion. Other research shows that people in Western societies are becoming more self-centred and narcissistic. But a major key to happiness is maintaining healthy relationships around us by thinking of others' needs. For the next week, focus on doing something small for someone else every day. Try it and see how good you feel.

'Ask not what your country can do for you –
ask what you can do for your country.'
– JOHN F KENNEDY

59. Let others brag for you

Bragging about our achievements is a common drive, but you can easily risk offending others by showing that you think you are better than them. Remember, happy relationships are integral for a happy life. The next time you want to brag to others about your achievements or highlight how much you know (this includes on social media), pause. Let your actions speak louder than words and go easy on the self-praise in public. If you won't brag about your achievements, then it's likely others will want to be identified with you and brag on your behalf. This is the best type of bragging.

'Boasting is one of those rare outfits that never looks good on you, but makes you look stunning when modeled by your admirers.'
– Richelle E Goodrich

60. Examine your relationships

It's not relationships, but *healthy* relationships, that are the vital ingredient for happiness. We often fall into the trap of hanging on to unhealthy friendships because they're familiar. Have you been consistently let down by a friend or partner, but justify their behaviour by telling yourself that it's just their personality? If you're the one putting in all the work, then you may need to re-examine the relationship. Like having an immunisation shot to fend off disease, ending a relationship may be initially painful, but the long-term benefit will outweigh the temporary discomfort. What relationships in your life need re-examining?

'If you're giving your all to someone and it's not enough, you're giving it to the wrong person.'

— AUTHOR UNKNOWN

ANTHONY GUNN

61. Dieting or lie-eting

We all know that diets don't work over time. You
may lose weight at the start of a diet, but the weight
will quickly come back. When you repeatedly diet,
the body gets used to being starved so it conserves
fat and is less willing to let go of it. When diets
don't work and the weight is put back on, people
feel like failures, which risks lowering happiness.
From now on, forget the term diet, and replace it
with 'life change'. What life changes can you make
around food? Maybe it's having healthy snacks
you can easily get to, cooking healthy meals and
keeping them in the freezer for evenings when you
don't have time to cook, having healthy breakfasts
or not keeping treats in the cupboard. Weight can
play a significant role in one's happiness levels. Give
yourself the best chance of success by forgetting
diets and focusing on life change.

*'I've been on a diet for two weeks
and all I've lost is two weeks.'*

— TOTIE FIELDS

62. Be aware of people's number-one fear

People's number-one fear, more than dying, is fear of rejection. It's a hardwired fear that our ancestors have passed on because if they were kicked out of the tribe or clan, it meant certain death. Even though this fear isn't as important today, it still affects our lives. You can, however, overcome the fear of rejection. Notice the times you're needlessly doing things to impress others instead of yourself. Awareness is the key to change. When we feel comfortable being ourselves instead of trying to be someone we're not, our lives become a lot more relaxed and we become happier people.

'Tension is who you think you should be. Relaxation is who you are.'

— CHINESE PROVERB

63. What legacy are you leaving behind?

Often we think of a legacy as something amazing and special. Yet, a legacy can also be negative. The parent who doesn't take care of their health or can't show affection to their kids, the person who blames everyone else for their problems, the person who frequently drinks to excess as a way to unwind are all leaving a legacy. If you have tremendous talent in an area but do nothing with it, then you too are leaving a legacy. Feed your happiness by choosing a legacy you'll be proud of.

'Your story is the greatest legacy that you will leave to your friends. It's the longest-lasting legacy you will leave to your heirs.'

— STEVE SAINT

64. Have a pre-planned calendar

Trying to plan enjoyable things to do a day or two beforehand or, worse, on the day, can be difficult. Why? Because if we are feeling down or exhausted, our minds can't think creatively. It's better to plan future events when you're feeling good. Even if you aren't feeling motivated before doing the activity, you'll feel much better by the end of it. What can you do with family or friends in the coming weeks and months? Put it in writing. Also, tell people about your future plans and you'll be making a public commitment, which will be further motivation to ensure you follow through with your plans. Remember, happy people plan future activities in advance. If it's on the calendar then do it, regardless of how you're feeling at the time. How can you fill in your calendar?

'Every time you tear a leaf off a calendar,
you present a new place for new ideas and progress.'
— CHARLES KETTERING

65. Be careful who you seek advice from

Have you ever shared your dream, only to be told all the reasons why you'll fail? People can be quick to tell us the reasons we'll fail at going back to study, finding another job, making a major purchase or trying something new. Sadly, many people often feel threatened by others' achievements. One simple way to know who to share your ideas with is to think about how successful the person is. Quite often, if they have already achieved success in life, they'll feel less threatened by your desire to succeed, and instead want to motivate you. Negative people will steal your dreams, and your happiness. Be warned.

'Don't follow any advice, no matter how good, until you feel as deeply in your spirit as you think in your mind that the counsel is wise.'
— JOAN RIVERS

66. Question your initial impulse

Psychologists from the University of Glasgow discovered that people make an assumption on trustworthiness within the first half a second of hearing a stranger's voice. We are quick to judge others, ourselves and situations, but these initial judgements are often wrong. Responding without thinking can be disastrous. People often let opportunities go because they are guided by the judgemental part of their brains. Before you respond to what you see as a problem, pause. Your initial reaction might be wrong and may rob you of happiness.

'Before you speak, listen. Before you write, think.
Before you spend, earn. Before you invest, investigate.
Before you criticize, wait. Before you pray, forgive. Before
you quit, try. Before you retire, save. Before you die, give.'
— WILLIAM ARTHUR WARD

67. Look after your reputation

Research shows that humans are quick to judge others, and if that judgement is negative, opinions can be hard to change. It's believed this is an evolutionary adaptation passed on from our early ancestors. If a person acted dishonestly or dishonourably back then, the safety of the rest of the tribe or clan could be threatened. If you develop a reputation as being untrustworthy, you may be ostracised. People who are ostracised have been shown to suffer from more health issues and even have a shorter life. The take-home message is this: look after your reputation by leading a decent life and you'll be looking after your happiness.

'It takes 20 years to build a reputation and five minutes to ruin it. If you think about that, you'll do things differently.'
— WARREN BUFFETT

68. Take responsibility for your life

I once provided therapy to people who had just been released from prison. What amazed me was that some believed it was everyone else's fault that they had ended up in jail or had no money or failed in relationships. Before you righteously nod your head in agreement, know that everyone is susceptible to this flaw, including you. Blaming others feels good but won't get you anywhere as it diminishes your sense of control. Yes, bad things outside our control can happen, but we have control over how we react. The moment we take responsibility and stop blaming others we can focus on finding a solution. Take responsibility for your life and you'll be taking responsibility for your happiness.

'We are all self-made, but only the successful will admit it.'
— EARL NIGHTINGALE

69. Invest in your education

By reading this book you are investing in yourself. Research shows that a person's income increases in proportion to the amount of time spent getting an education. Yes, it will seem like hard work and sacrifice. And yes, you may feel like it's too late in life to go back to study. But you're going to age anyway, so you may as well do it with an education. What's more, having an education is empowering. Go on: invest in yourself and your happiness.

'Why get an education? How do you convince anyone you are worth anything if you don't invest in yourself?'

— DANIELLE BABB

70. Make your bathroom a classroom

Did you know that the tensor tympani muscle is located within the ear and helps dampen sounds such as those made by chewing, so we don't deafen ourselves? Most of us know little about our internal world: our bodies. A fun and simple way to help remedy this is to get an anatomy poster of the human body and hang it in your bathroom. You could do the same with a poster of the world, our solar system or maths problems. Each time you visit your bathroom you'll be getting an education, and education gives empowerment. Now that's something to get happy about.

*'The whole purpose of education
is to turn mirrors into windows.'*
– Sydney J Harris

71. Defuse your ticking time bomb

Many of us have a ticking time bomb in our lives, waiting to explode. Yet we ignore it, hoping it will go away. The problem with putting your head in the sand is that the issue only gets worse. It's like ignoring weeds in a garden, hoping they'll disappear by themselves. Deep down, we often know when we are deceiving ourselves, and our happiness suffers as a result. What's the ticking time bomb in your life? Starting today, what steps can you take to start defusing your time bomb?

'The first wealth is health.'
— Ralph Waldo Emerson

72. Become a deep-breathing expert

When we become stressed we often fail to breathe properly. This disrupts the oxygen levels in our blood, causing tightness and pain in the chest, dizziness, a racing heart and panic symptoms. Deep breathing is a simple strategy you can use to lower stress levels. Practise breathing in for three seconds, feeling your lower abdomen expand like a balloon; hold for three seconds; then breathe out for three seconds and feel your lower abdomen deflate. Do this for three minutes while you're doing something mindless. The more you practise, the more natural it will be to use during times of high stress. Deep breathing is cheap insurance against unhappiness.

*'If you want to conquer the anxiety of life,
live in the moment, live in the breath.'*
– AMIT RAY

73. Be aware of 'thought–action fusion'

A common psychological phenomenon is believing that thinking about a bad event can make it come true. This is known as thought–action fusion. At a recent workshop, the presenter asked a room of psychologists to imagine a person they loved and then to write out the following sentence with their name in the space: 'I hope _____ is in a car accident.'

I was there and I don't think there was a psychologist in the room who didn't feel squeamish. Then we were told to write out the following sentence with the same loved one's name: 'I hope _____ wins the lottery.'

The room erupted into laughter as no-one believed that would come true. We tend to believe our thoughts can make bad events happen, but are less likely to make positive events happen. Our primal brains are hardwired to pay more attention to being worried than happy. Remember this the next time your worries try to overtake your happiness.

'Negative thoughts stick around because we believe them, not because we want them or choose them.'

— ANDREW BERNSTEIN

74. Your thoughts are just thoughts

Believing our thoughts fuse into actions is a common thinking trap for a variety of mental health disorders. Do you believe that thinking something (or even worse, saying the thought out loud) could make a negative event come true? Thought–action fusion is one of the best examples to show how we can be a prisoner to our thoughts. The next time you feel apprehensive because you have a certain thought, tell yourself that this is simply the primal part of your brain obsessing over risk. Before you react to your brain's oversensitive alarm about harm, take ten deep breaths. This will ground you and let the rational part of your brain speak up. Your thoughts are just thoughts – they can't harm you. Now breathe and let your happiness grow.

*'There are more things to alarm us
than to harm us, and we suffer more
often in apprehension than reality.'*

— SENECA

75. Practise betting on yourself

Before bookies accept bets at horse races, they first decide on the likelihood of a particular horse winning. The better the chance a horse has of winning, the lower the odds, and the less money you will make if your horse wins. Bookies understand they don't have control over the result, which is why they'll give the odds or the probability of a horse winning. Unlike bookies, we often believe we are 100 per cent accurate in predicting what will happen to us in the future: *I will fail the job interview; this cake I'm baking won't turn out; everyone will hate my speech.* For one week, act like a bookie and give yourself odds of the likelihood your worrisome predictions will come true. Write them down and then at the end of the week see how many actually came true. Realistic predictions about our future performance is at the core of happiness. What would you be like as a bookie if you were to place odds on yourself?

'Never make predictions,
especially about the future.'
— CASEY STENGEL

76. What do you already have?

One day a young monk was walking home when he came to the banks of a flooded river. Staring hopelessly, he suddenly saw a great teacher on the other side of the river. The young monk yelled to the teacher, 'Oh, wise one, can you tell me how to get to the other side of this river?' The teacher pondered, looked up and down the river and yelled back, 'My son, you are on the other side.'

What do you already have that would make others happy if they had it?

'Be thankful for what you have;
you'll end up having more.
If you concentrate on what you don't have,
you will never, ever have enough.'

— OPRAH WINFREY

---

77. Before you point the blame, pause

King Henry VIII had six wives. He was desperate for an heir to his throne. When a wife gave him a daughter rather than a son, he'd replace her with another wife. Of these six wives one died of natural causes, one survived, two were divorced, and two were beheaded. King Henry blamed his wives for not being able to provide a son to inherit his throne; what's ironic is that, as we now know, it's the father who is responsible for determining the sex of a child. Anger and blame drain happiness. Before you point the blame at someone else, pause. Is there a chance that you may not have all the facts, or that your anger is obscuring your judgement?

'When you blame others,
you give up your power to change.'
– ROBERT ANTHONY

78. If you are bored, then focus on it

Have you ever had someone tell you, 'I'm bored'? Often, what this person is really saying is, 'Entertain me'. Yes, we need others for happiness, but relying solely on others to entertain you and relieve your boredom risks you becoming an addict. The moment you sense even remote feelings of boredom, you'll feel compelled to seek out others. What's the answer? Focus on your boredom and study your reaction to it: what thoughts are you having, how does your body feel, what is your posture like, is your breathing shallow and short? Focus on your boredom and you'll never be bored again.

'When you pay attention to boredom it gets unbelievably interesting.'
– Jon Kabat-Zinn

79. Develop psychological flexibility

A strong tree, if covered in snow, is likely to break under the weight. Yet a flimsy sapling that flattens under the snow will quickly spring back to its original height once the snow has melted. Be like the sapling and adapt to your surroundings by developing psychological flexibility: the ability to entertain new ways of thinking. Do you find yourself quick to judge others or, worse, quick to judge yourself? What are you rigidly convinced you could never achieve? Whatever it is, give it a go. Be flexible about what you can do and adapt to your environment. A flexible mind is a happy mind.

'Life is movement. The more life there is, the more flexibility there is. The more fluid you are, the more you are alive.'

— Arnaud Desjardins

80. Ask questions instead of arguing

This statement would seem in contrast to the popular advice on assertiveness. But arguing only serves to strengthen a person's belief. Even if they are shown to be wrong and they know it, a person will often still hold their position to save face. Instead of arguing, let go of having to be right. Act like a detective looking for facts: be genuinely interested, ask a person about their point of view and get them to explain it in depth. Just explaining our beliefs out loud can help us realise the flaws in them. Who knows, you may even change your mind too! Remember, a flexible mind is a happy mind.

'I'd far rather be happy than right any day.'
– Douglas Adams

81. Inflated responsibility

A person I once counselled believed they could predict earthquakes. As a result they felt it was their responsibility to travel to areas they believed were at risk, to warn people. As tragic as this case sounds, we often fall into a similar trap of believing we are responsible for things outside our control. Generally we aren't bothered by things that aren't personally meaningful to us; the things we care about make us stressed and anxious. What areas do you have an inflated sense of responsibility for? Do you really have control over them?

'There is only one cause of unhappiness:
the false beliefs you have in your head,
beliefs so widespread, so commonly held,
that it never occurs to you to question them.'
– ANTHONY DE MELLO

---

82. Make a 'control contract' with yourself

If we do naturally want to take control of things that are personally meaningful to us, even when they're outside our control, what can be done? One tip is to make yourself aware of this control bias by creating a contract with yourself and determining the level of responsibility you should take on. Regularly reminding yourself to focus on controlling things within your control is at the heart of happiness. Fill in the following contract and place a copy on the fridge so it's clearly visible.

I ....

agree to accept ....% responsibility for things

that happen outside my control today.

Signed,

....

*'The first principle of contract negotiations
is don't remind them of what you did in the past –
tell them what you're going to do in the future.'*

– STAN MUSIAL

83. Avoid using the four-letter word

We talk to ourselves at over 500 words per minute, with the vast majority of this internal chatter being negative. One toxic word that can be disastrous for our happiness is 'can't'. It steals our belief in ourselves: *I can't write, I can't do sport, I can't cook, I can't play chess, I can't* (fill in the blank). Often it's not that we can't do something, but rather that we're put off by how we might perform if we attempt it. Give this experiment a go. For the next three days, whenever you notice yourself saying you *can't* do something, drop the 't'. Yes, you may not be able to do it well initially, due to a lack of experience, but you will be able to do it. Give it a go: drop the 't' and see what you *can* achieve.

> *'Knock the "t" off the can't.'*
> – GEORGE REEVES

84. Be careful of shoulds

Another toxic word that can make us angry and irritable is the word 'should': for example, *they should know I'm on a diet; I should not be treated like this; I should produce excellent work every time.* Angry people often have an irrational belief that the world *should* follow their wishes. Shoulds promote a fixed and inflexible belief of how the world operates. Adopt flexible thinking and lower the perfectionist, fixed view of how the world needs to operate. Remember, flexible thinking is central to happiness. What *shoulds* can you drop from your life?

'Being happy doesn't mean that everything is perfect. It means that you've decided to look beyond the imperfections.'
– GERARD WAY

85. I have to ...

Do you ever use the phrase, 'I have to'? *I have to lose weight, I have to look after everyone else's needs before my own, I have to work in this job.* The only things you truly have to do are eat, sleep and breathe. Apart from this, virtually everything else is a choice. Granted, at times the choice may seem non-existent, but it's still a choice. The reason we use such a phrase as 'I have to' is that it helps us believe we have no control, thereby excusing us from taking personal responsibility for our lives. Take back control of your happiness and replace 'I have to' with 'I choose to'. It's a small change, but a powerful one.

'If it's never our fault, we can't take responsibility for it. If we can't take responsibility for it, we'll always be its victim.'

– RICHARD BACH

---

86. Shock your senses

Nothing is quite as effective in knocking a person out of their slumbering life as an extreme change. This doesn't have to be as extreme as bungee jumping or moving overseas. It does, however, need to involve shocking your senses. For example, breathe through a straw, eat a small piece of chilli or have someone tip a bucket of icy water over you. The discomfort will make your senses come alive and flush any fogginess from your head. Not only will it make you feel alive thanks to a surge of adrenalin and feel-good endorphins, but it will also make you more appreciative of the comforts you have. There's nothing like being freezing and then standing in front of a heater to increase your happiness. Go on, shock your senses.

'Happiness is a state of activity.'
– ARISTOTLE

87. Treat your happiness like your teeth

Did you know that the average person spends 38.5 days brushing their teeth over a lifetime? You can't brush your teeth just once and then expect them to be fine for the rest of your life; your teeth need daily maintenance to ensure they function well. As with your teeth, your happiness also needs regular maintenance through daily activities to ensure its longevity. What can you do today to maintain your happiness?

'Happiness is not a station you arrive at, but a manner of traveling.'
— MARGARET LEE RUNBECK

88. What are you letting get away from you?

Many of us lead busy lives. Time can seem to get away from us, due to work, family or other pressures. Yet there is a price for everything we do. Potentially the most toxic emotion of all is regret, and many people in later life look back and have regrets about what they wished they'd done. What are you letting get away from you? Maybe it's your kids, friendships, hobbies, your health or your education. Avoid regrets and put the important things first. Your future happiness depends on it.

'The main thing is to keep the main thing the main thing.'

– STEPHEN R COVEY

89. Will your dreams make you a victim?

Contestants on TV singing competitions will often passionately explain how all they want to do is sing. Placing everything on one dream in life poses two problems: first, your dream may not come true, and second, if it does, then you may have put all your focus on that one endeavour and have nothing else. Sadly, this is why many performers, regardless of whether they make it, become bitter and disillusioned. Athletes who are dropped from a team, workaholics who lose their job, or performers who are no longer sought after are at a high risk of mental illness. There has to be more to you than one area, otherwise your happiness is dependent on luck.

'Remember that sometimes not getting what you want is a wonderful stroke of luck.'
– DALAI LAMA

90. The perfect job rarely exists

After spending years training to be a psychologist and completing a PhD, I should be in my dream job. Yet I still fantasise about my earlier plans to become a builder. Be careful not to fall into the trap of thinking that your career has to be perfect. Follow a passion, but if you're hoping that a career will give your life total meaning, your life is guaranteed to be empty. If you find a job that gives you happiness, then I congratulate you. But look for other areas to complement your happiness.

'Most people I know who were sure of their career path at 20 are having midlife crises now.'
– TIM MINCHIN

91. Pause before pressing send

Confrontation is a major fear for most people because it taps into our number-one fear: rejection. This evolutionary fear is one of the reasons why people find it easier to be confrontational via text or email, as it negates the need for face-to-face contact. Don't allow yourself to be tempted by this seemingly simple way out. It's like firing a long-range missile: just because you aren't there to directly see the impact, it doesn't mean damage isn't being inflicted. What's worse, once it's in writing, a person can keep re-reading your hurtful words. Once you've written a message, sleep on it before sending it. Pause before pressing the send button and ask yourself if this is really a battle worth fighting. Avoiding unnecessary conflict will reap dividends for your happiness.

'An injury is much sooner forgotten than an insult.'

– PHILIP STANHOPE

92. Have a 'no-screen day'

As TVs, mobile phones and other devices become an integral part of our lives, it's becoming more difficult for people in developed countries to go a day without sitting in front of some type of screen. Screens have their benefits, but they are also highly addictive and often prevent a person from getting out and engaging with life. Try this challenge: for one day have a no-screen day. It's likely you'll initially go through withdrawal symptoms and won't know how to entertain yourself. Stay strong, as these feelings will pass. There's no greater sense of accomplishment than testing ourselves through discomfort and boredom, and knowing we can cope.

'The two enemies of human happiness are pain and boredom.'

– ARTHUR SCHOPENHAUER

93. Cut back on screen time

I've counselled many people who suffered from insomnia. Upon further questioning, I've often found their sleep issues were a result of being addicted to checking social media. Social media can be great for keeping in contact with friends and family, but too much of it has been shown to lead to mental health issues. Give your happiness a chance and have set times where you turn off your electronic devices.

'It takes discipline not to let social media steal your time.'
– ALEXIS OHANIAN

94. Know when to quit

A common piece of advice that successful people will freely chant is to never quit. However, there are probably just as many people who have stuck with a problem and failed, not because of lack of trying, but because they didn't know when to walk away. Whether it's leaving an unhealthy relationship or career, moving house or replacing a sport, hobby or interest with a different one, look for the following signals to determine if it's time to quit:

- Your wellbeing is suffering.
- It's taking time from more rewarding endeavours.
- You can't see a possible solution by continuing.
- You're staying with it more through fear than faith.

Knowing when to quit is never easy, but if it's affecting your long-term happiness, then the decision may have been made for you.

'If you must play, decide on three things
at the start: the rules of the game,
the stakes, and the quitting time.'

– CHINESE PROVERB

95. What type of stress is in your life?

Not all stress is bad. There are two types of stress: negative stress, or distress, has been associated with a variety of diseases and even premature death; positive stress, known as eustress, is linked with increased health. What is the difference? Put simply, negative stress is caused by high demands with low control, while positive stress is the opposite. Examples of negative stress are losing your job due to a downturn in the market, a loved one being injured or becoming ill, or running late for a flight due to traffic. Positive stress is where you have control; this may include starting a new job, getting married, buying a home or car, or pushing yourself through exercise to attain a goal. The key here is not stress but the level of control you feel you have over a situation. Stress is good provided you feel a realistic sense of control over the circumstances. Once the sense of control goes, then our happiness is likely to follow.

'… there is no progress without eustress,
and the more eustress we can create
or apply to our lives, the sooner
we can actualize our dreams.'
— TIM FERRISS

96. Are you a victim or a survivor?

If control is the fundamental ingredient that regulates whether stress is positive or negative, it's important to identify areas where you either do or don't have control. Often, unhappy people who harbour a victim mentality will focus on what they can't control. Ask yourself how much time you are giving to the areas you can't control compared to the areas you can control.

'Victims focus on what they do not control. Survivors focus on what they do control.'
— KEVIN M GILMARTIN

97. Capture opportunities

Successful people often attribute their lucky break to a time they were at a crossroad and decided to act: for example, being offered a new job or opportunity and taking it. If an unsuccessful person were faced with the same situation, it's likely they'd choose the option of making no decision, and fail to act. Opportunities can often be disguised, such as being invited to a social event and meeting someone who later has a big influence on your life. Capture opportunities when they come, because it's often the ones we are initially hesitant to embrace that can send our lives in positive new directions.

'If you had one shot, or one opportunity to seize everything you ever wanted, one moment, would you capture it or just let it slip?'
— EMINEM

98. Practise random acts of kindness

Going to church as a young boy on a Sunday, I would be amazed at how people were caring towards others during the service, but the moment it was over there was a rush to be the first out of the church car park. Saying nice things to others is good, but it pales in comparison to performing acts of kindness for others. Not only that, performing an act of kindness for another person is guaranteed to boost your happiness by helping your body release feel-good endorphins. It might be letting someone with fewer items go before you at a checkout, helping someone who looks lost or is struggling with a load, or sending a positive email to someone congratulating them on something they have done (or sending it to their boss and copying them in on it). What random act of kindness can you perform today?

'A thousand words will not leave so deep an impression as one deed.'

— Henrik Ibsen

99. Prevention is better than cure

'Don't sweat the small stuff' has become a popular saying, and it has a lot of merit. However, one drawback of this advice is it can encourage people to ignore small problems by only focusing on the big problems. Often it's the small problems that manifest into bigger issues, a bit like scratching yourself and dismissing it as nothing, only to have the scratch become seriously infected. Whether it's not getting the mechanic to look at the noise in your car, only to later have the engine fail; sitting too long at the computer without getting up and stretching, resulting in serious pain; or not keeping up to date with an insurance policy and then being unable to make a claim, it's often the small but preventable things that grow into disasters. By the time there's a breakage, it's too late. Instead, look for strains to prevent breakages – it's an important key for happiness.

'Prevention is better than cure.'

— DESIDERIUS ERASMUS

100. Suppression turns into obsession

Try this experiment: for one minute you're not allowed to think of a white elephant. Go on, attempt it.

How did you go? It's impossible to consciously not allow ourselves to think of a white elephant. Why? Because we have to first think of a white elephant to know not to think about it. The same happens when trying to suppress any type of thought. Our thoughts can't hurt us as they are only thoughts, no matter how negative. Yet the more you suppress the thought and try not to think about it, the stronger it becomes. For real happiness, be friends with the unwanted thought, allow it to be, observe it, and watch its power over you drop.

'When you suppress your darkness
you also suppress your light.'
— BRYANT MCGILL

101. Are you a control freak?

Many people I see for counselling diagnose themselves as control freaks. They feel the need to be in charge to ensure everything is done properly. Whether you're unwilling to delegate jobs, to allow your partner to choose your child's clothes, or to be a passenger in a car, 24/7 control is both hard work and draining. Lower your guard a little, starting with the small things. Let your young child butter their own toast, leave the bed unmade for a day, delegate a job, or ask for help if you wouldn't normally. Even if things didn't go as well as if you'd done them yourself, was the outcome as bad as you had predicted? Try giving up control of the little things in life and let your happiness breathe.

'Sometimes the best control is giving up control.'
– Todd Fleischer and Jerry Bockoven

---

102. Kill the will to spend

Retail therapy is a misnomer. Buying new things is unlikely to make us happy for long. This is because of habituation – we get used to things quickly. Going into debt to buy objects with the assumption that they'll make us happier seldom works. Before you lash out and buy that new object with the belief you'll never want again, pause. Instead, go and visit a friend, travel somewhere new or go for a walk. Not only will you save money, but it will be better for your happiness.

'He who buys what he does not need
steals from himself.'
— SWEDISH PROVERB

103. Who is your support group?

Did you know that lonely people have more health problems and a shorter life span than people who have a strong social network? Humans are herd animals; we need others. Having a support group for illness, addiction, sport, hobbies, business or your social life can be beneficial. It's vital to have a group of people you can bounce ideas off, or get advice and gain general support from. Who is your support group? If you don't have one, what group could you look at joining? Happiness comes from feeling supported.

'Friends are the family you choose.'
– Jess C Scott

104. Are you keeping hydrated?

Our bodies are made up of about 75 per cent water, and the average adult loses approximately 2.5 to 3 litres of water per day. When our body's water levels drop too much we become dehydrated, causing headaches and lethargy, the body's way of making us slow down to conserve water. Unfortunately, you can't count on your body's thirst mechanisms to protect you because by the time you notice you're thirsty, you're already slightly dehydrated. The answer is to make sure you have water nearby whenever possible and take regular sips throughout the day. Not only will staying hydrated ensure your energy lasts longer, but you'll also be healthier and happier for it.

'Thousands have lived without love,
not one without water.'
– WH Auden

105. Screen the caffeine

Caffeine is so potent and addictive that if it were discovered today you'd probably need a prescription to buy it. The body's response to caffeine can mimic an adrenalin rush or even a panic attack, and while it takes up to twenty minutes to take effect, it can last for over six hours. If you suffer from stress or panic attacks, or have trouble sleeping, look at your caffeine intake. Cut back and your body will thank you. If you feel nervous about cutting back, that's more reason to look at your caffeine as a problem that is affecting your happiness.

'Learn to let go.
That is the key to happiness.'
— BUDDHA

106. Is your home a decorated prison?

Thanks to home improvement TV shows, we're taught that a highly decorated house equals happiness. It's good to be house proud, but like anything in life there needs to be balance. Do you really need to get into further debt to make your house look nicer? Is there a chance you might be trying to keep up with the neighbours? A house is designed to be a safe place we can return to after having adventures. Ask yourself, is your home like a prison that prevents you from getting out to explore and experience life?

'Are these things really better than the things I already have? Or am I just trained to be dissatisfied with what I have now?'
— Lullaby, Chuck Palahniuk

107. How are you comparing yourself with others?

We naturally compare ourselves with others in either an upward or a downward direction. Comparing ourselves with others above us can be good if we are aspiring to be like an elite athlete, musician, entrepreneur or cook. However, upward social comparison with those who we believe have a better job, physical looks, car or home will lower our happiness levels. Happy people have been shown to compare themselves more with people who are worse off, which is known as downward social comparison. For example, visiting a cancer hospital will make a healthy person realise how fortunate their life is and want to make the most of it. Are you comparing yourself with others in an upward or downward direction?

'Jealousy is the fear of comparison.'
— MAX FRISCH

108. Choose optimism

Optimistic people are generally more cheerful and happy, are more resilient, adapt better to failures and hardships, are less likely to develop depression, have stronger immune systems, take better care of their health, and are even more likely to live longer. Try this challenge: tell your friends, family or work colleagues that for the next week they have to point out every time you are not being optimistic. If you're really serious, have a jar in which you have to put a set amount of money each time you're pessimistic. At the end of the week the money in the jar goes to charity. Try it and watch what happens to your happiness levels.

'If you were allowed one wish for your child, seriously consider wishing him or her optimism.'
— DANIEL KAHNEMAN

109. Offer empathy before advice

There's an old saying that we have two ears and one mouth so we can listen twice as much as we speak. People often overlook this recommendation when another person mentions their problems. Other people's problems make us uncomfortable, so we try to fix them to get rid of our discomfort instead of empathising and listening. Not only do you leave yourself open to be blamed if your unsolicited advice doesn't work, but you're also robbing the other person of control. If you want to make someone truly happy, sit with your discomfort and just listen. Then, if they ask for your advice, you can offer it. Offer empathy before advice and watch what it does to another person's happiness.

'Avoid giving advice unless it's asked for.'
– GLENN DAVIS

110. Treat your brain along with your pain

The brain doesn't feel pain because brain tissue doesn't contain pain receptors. This is why neurosurgeons can perform brain surgery while the patient is awake. Yet, 100 per cent of pain the body experiences is produced by the brain. Nothing can attack happiness faster than a painful injury that prevents you from leading your normal life. The brain will sometimes keep producing pain long after an injury has repaired, in an attempt to protect the body. The treatment is to retrain the brain by gradually becoming more physically active. This is why health professionals often want a person to start rehabilitating an injury as soon as possible, even if it hurts. If you are suffering from pain, seek professional advice. Don't let your brain make you a prisoner to pain; your happiness depends on it.

'Do not confuse my bad days as a sign of weakness.
Those are actually the days I'm fighting my hardest.'

— AUTHOR UNKNOWN

111. Recovery involves setting small goals

The physical limitations and pain caused by an injury can be disastrous for happiness. I spoke with one person who is all too familiar with injury, Glenn Kearney, a world-class enduro-motorcross champion. Despite all his international victories, Glenn has faced considerable pain and setbacks due to serious injuries caused by racing. Interestingly, Glenn uses his competitive nature and focused attention for achieving goals to help in recovering from injuries. With the help of his health professionals, Glenn breaks down his long-term goal, to be back racing by a certain time, by setting himself small, achievable tasks. Being injured can rob anyone of happiness. It's important to take back control and set small, realistic goals for your recovery so you can keep your motivation high. With your health professional, map out your recovery plan and take small steps towards achieving your goal.

'On particularly rough days when I'm sure I can't possibly endure, I like to remind myself that my track record for getting through bad days so far is 100%.'

— VINNY GENOVESI

112. Be selfish by helping others

Mother Teresa did some amazing, selfless charity work in her life, though some psychologists have said that her altruistic efforts may have been motivated by self-interest. How? When we help people it feels good because our bodies release feel-good endorphins. Whether you're doing volunteer work, coaching a team, helping at the local school, organising a fundraiser for charity or helping a person who is lost, knowing you have had a positive impact on another person's life is a sure way of putting a smile on your face. Today, look for a way to be selfish by helping someone in need and notice the feeling it gives you.

'Cultivating the habit of good deeds will not only affect those around us, it will improve our own emotional well being.'
— Debbie Macomber

113. Let people help you

It feels good to help someone in need. Likewise, seeing a person's face light up as you give them a present they've longed for can be equally satisfying. Even though we are aware of this, many of us fail to see how allowing others to help us is giving them this same experience. It may be something as small as asking someone for directions and then thanking them for their help, or accepting a gift after you've lent your neighbour the lawnmower. Allowing a person to genuinely help you can increase their happiness. By accepting help, you are in turn giving them an invaluable gift. Think of it as an act of kindness. That's something to get happy about.

*'Help others achieve their dreams
and you will achieve yours.'*
– LES BROWN

114. Be aware of the nocebo effect

Give a person a plain sugar pill, but tell them it reduces pain. If after taking it they believe they feel less pain, this positive influence is an example of the placebo effect. The negative influences from the nocebo effect are not well known. A person dying after being told they've been cursed with voodoo magic is one example of the nocebo effect. Likewise, if you rub harmless cream on a person's skin and tell them it contains poison ivy, their skin may break out in a rash. The nocebo effect works because the human brain is very susceptible to negative suggestion from others. What negative things have others told you that you now believe will come true? Think carefully before accepting someone else's negative prediction for you, as the nocebo effect feeds on happiness.

'Good advice is often annoying –
bad advice never is.'

– FRENCH PROVERB

115. Practise making quick decisions

Indecision can be crippling, because we overestimate the risk of making a wrong decision. This is why many people get others to make decisions for them: *I'll have whatever you decide*; *Do you think we should go to the movies?*; *Do you think this top matches these pants?* Making quick decisions is a habit that can be learned. For one week, focus on making quick decisions. Try these exercises:

- Travel to a new area and explore different routes.
- Order the first thing that gets your attention on a menu.
- Buy the first item you see on a supermarket shelf if there is a large variety of brands.

Start training to make quick decisions today. You'll be amazed at not only how quickly you can master it, but also what it does for your happiness.

*'The risk of a wrong decision
is preferable to the terror of indecision.'*
— MAIMONIDES

116. Know your happiness clock

Happiness levels naturally fluctuate throughout the day based on a person's energy levels. Energy levels are often at their lowest in the early morning and late evening, and heightened around the middle of the day. Things that can help boost energy, and therefore your happiness, include exercise, adequate sleep, being hydrated, avoiding fatty foods and big meals that require a lot of energy to digest, and avoiding sunburn. However, expecting to be overly happy and full of energy all the time may not be realistic; know that energy levels can fluctuate throughout the day, and be kind to yourself in your quest for greater happiness.

'Eat when you're hungry. Drink when you're thirsty. Sleep when you're tired.'
— BUDDHIST PROVERB

117. Treat intrusive thoughts as visitors

Of all the different types of intrusive thoughts people have, do you know the most common type? Researchers have found it is self-doubt: *Am I just an imposter in this job?*; *Did I really lock the front door?*; *I'm not smart enough to apply for the course*; *Why would they want to associate with me?* Next time you have a self-doubting thought, instead of believing it, identify it as an intrusive thought. The thought can be there; you just don't have to believe it. Like training a muscle, practice will make it easier to handle self-doubting thoughts. Make up your mind to treat intrusive thoughts as passing visitors instead of welcomed guests, and your happiness will grow exponentially.

'Most people are about as happy as they make up their minds to be.'
– Abraham Lincoln

118. Play like a child

Children have a natural ability to gain enjoyment from the smallest things. Whether they're playing with a stick, jumping in puddles or trying to catch leaves blowing in the wind, kids have fun when they play. Playing provides the perfect environment for learning. If you want a rush of feel-good endorphins, play like a child by trying any of the following:

- Go on a swing.
- Jump in a puddle.
- Run through a water sprinkler.
- Skip in public.
- Camp out in the backyard.
- Cook marshmallows on an open fire.
- Dance at home to music.
- Go on rides at a theme park.

Today, play like a child and I guarantee you'll learn something new about happiness.

*'We don't stop playing because we grow old;
we grow old because we stop playing.'*
– GEORGE BERNARD SHAW

119. Discomfort creates new neural pathways

Mastering a new skill requires new neural pathways in the brain. However, until these pathways are properly formed, there will be discomfort. This is why people often quit a new task after barely giving it a go – it's too uncomfortable so the new neural pathways never develop. This often leaves you believing you are dumb or uncoordinated. Try this challenge. Write your first name on a piece of paper. Now write your name again but with your non-dominant hand. How did you go? It probably felt uncomfortable the second time. Write your name with your non-dominant hand thirty times. Now compare your thirtieth attempt to the attempt made with your dominant hand. It will probably be similar. Allowing yourself to feel discomfort as you create new neural pathways is the key to learning any new skill. Sit with the discomfort and you will surprise yourself with what you achieve and feel happier for it.

'Do not wait to strike till the iron is hot;
but make it hot by striking.'

– WILLIAM B YEATS

120. You'll forget this page within a week, unless …

You have now finished this book, but simply having read the pages without putting the suggestions into practice probably won't help you achieve lasting happiness. What helps make things concrete in our minds is physical experience, as it creates new neural pathways in the brain. One of the best ways to remember information is to test yourself. If you want to remember a happiness strategy from this book, test yourself by applying the technique to your everyday life. Even better, share a happiness strategy with a close friend and attempt it together. Go back through the book, select a single happiness strategy and try it. If it feels awkward at first, that's fine. You're creating new neural pathways in your brain. Keep at it until the discomfort drops – and it will! Treat your happiness like a muscle and exercise it regularly. Now, which happiness strategy will you attempt first?

'Tell me and I forget.
Teach me and I remember.
Involve me and I learn.'

— Benjamin Franklin

Acknowledgements

Jonathan Dyer, thanks for helping me create another book; Mel, my wife and best friend, and my children, Emma and Patrick; my agent Sally Bird; Fran Berry and the team from Hardie Grant Books, for giving me another opportunity; my editors, Rachel Day and Brooke Clark, for taking this book to a whole new level; Kylie Lyons from Handprint Photography; my parents, Ron and Helen; my parents-in-law, Bruce and Cynthya; my big brother Mick and his family, Leanne, Ben, Jade and Mitchell; my brother Ian and his family Nikki and Georgia; my sister Kazz and her family, Adrian, Zack, Ivy and Charlie; David Thorold, my 'Uncle D' in New Guinea, his wife Sal and their daughter Sophia; my cousins Mary-Anne, Ron and Ollie and their families; Uncle Barry and Aunty Rhonda, Dean, Glenn and Ben – thanks, Glenn, for sharing your knowledge and time with me for this book; Uncle Ron and Aunty Dee, Reece and Jarrod; Uncle Neil, Brent and Sarah; my grandmother, Marie Thorold, and Aunty Anne, who are in our hearts forever; and Gordon Pendlebury, the way you have handled your tragic loss is an inspiration to all.

About the author

Dr Anthony Gunn is a psychologist who doesn't have a history of being happy 24/7. The psychology of happiness, together with claims that a person's happiness can be increased, is what attracted Anthony to see if these techniques would work on him. To test these scientific claims about happiness, Anthony put his scepticism to the side and was surprised by the results … the happiness techniques actually worked. If you would like to increase your happiness, but are sceptical it can be done, then you're in good company. Prepare to be pleasantly proved wrong with this no-nonsense approach, and get happy!

Anthony's publications include *Swing High: Life Lessons from Childhood*, *Walk Tall: 100 Ways to Live Life to the Fullest* and *Raising Confident Happy Children: 40 tips for helping your child succeed*.

For more info go to: www.anthonygunn.com